Shrines of Sapporo, Japan

A TRAVEL PHOTO ART BOOK

LAINE CUNNINGHAM

Shrines of Sapporo, Japan

A Travel Photo Art Book

Published by Sun Dogs Creations
Changing the World One Book at a Time
Print ISBN: 978-1-951389-31-4

Cover Image by Laine Cunningham
Cover Design by Angel Leya

Copyright © 2023 Laine Cunningham

All rights reserved. No part of this book may be reproduced in any form or by any means, electronic, mechanical, digital, photocopying or recording, except for the inclusion in a review, without permission in writing from the publisher.

At Shinto shrines throughout Japan, straw ropes called shimenawa hang on trees and doorways to mark the boundaries of the sacred space. Banners called nobori line walkways to ease the transition out of the everyday bustle into a meditative realm. Single purple banners often identify the temple. And, of course, iconic torii gates of stone or wood mark the entrances.

In Sapporo, the three deities honored at the Hokkaido Shrine are Sukunahikona, Ookunitama, and Ookuninushi. The site, located in Maruyama Park, is festooned with fragrant pink blooms during the cherry blossom season's Golden Week. Grilling is only allowed in the park during this time, so take the opportunity to linger with local families.

A host of additional shrines are scattered throughout Sapporo's city and suburbs. Anyone can visit the resident gods, called kami. After cleansing yourself at the fountain, pause in front of the main hall. Bow twice, clap twice, and then clap once. Enjoy the calmness brought by this ritual to recharge for the next step on your journey.

BELLWETHER

LOTUS

BRIMFUL

CLEANSE

SEASONED

SKIRT

RUMPELSTILTSKIN

THREADING

STANDOFF

CHARMED

JANUS

GUARDIAN

ASSEMBLE

ASCENSION

AMIDST

PULSE

BEAK

WOOLLY

DAWNING

LIBERATION

TRACKS

AFLOAT

RHINO

RIMBAUD

ADVANCE

BEVELED

PEEKABOO

COURAGE

BASK

JETTY

RADIANT

BLENDE

AWAKE

PEACE

DISTINCT

EAGLE

MARQUE

BALE

VOGUE

KEEN

IMPERIAL

SLOOP

RECEIVER

COO

FADE

TITLES IN THIS SERIES

Gardens of Sapporo, Japan
Mt. Moiwa, Sapporo, Japan
Shinto Temples of Sapporo, Japan
Shrines of Sapporo, Japan
Parks of Sapporo, Japan
Sapporo City, Japan

www.ingramcontent.com/pod-product-compliance
Lightning Source LLC
Chambersburg PA
CBHW051359110526
44592CB00023B/2883